Unsettled Accounts

Unsettled Accounts

poems

Will Wells

OHIO UNIVERSITY PRESS

ATHENS

Ohio University Press, Athens, Ohio 45701
www.ohioswallow.com
© 2010 by Will Wells

To obtain permission to quote, reprint, or otherwise reproduce or distribute material
from Ohio University Press publications, please contact our rights and permissions
department at (740) 593-1154 or (740) 593-4536 (fax).

Printed in the United States of America
Ohio University Press books are printed on acid-free paper ⊚ ™

18 17 16 15 14 13 12 11 10   5 4 3 2 1

Library of Congress Cataloging-in-Publication Data
Wells, Will, 1952–
  Unsettled accounts : poems / Will Wells.
      p. cm.
  ISBN 978-0-8214-1903-8 (hc : alk. paper) — ISBN 978-0-8214-1904-5 (pbk. : alk.
paper) — ISBN 978-0-8214-4306-4 (electronic)
  I. Title.
  PS3623.E479U67 2010
  811'.6—dc22
                            2009046893

Acknowledgments

Grateful acknowledgment is made to the following publications in which these poems appeared, or are scheduled to appear (several in earlier versions):

Apalachee Quarterly: "Past Midnight, I Soak My Feet, Ravenna, 1317"
Birmingham Poetry Review: "Dirty Laundry"
Chicago Review: "Last Peaches, Chalfont St. Giles, 1665"
Cimarron Review: "Padova Pilgrimage" and "Ping-Pong with the Nazis"
Connecticut Review: "Indigo" and "Live Fire"
Denver Quarterly: "Hearing the Beat" originally "Upon Hearing a
    Recording of the Big Bang"
Envoi (U.K.): "Terrace on the Val Venosta" and "Young Retrievers:
    Near Oxford, 1973"
Field: "Spring Fever"
Gin Bender Poetry Review: "The Persistence of Memory: Houston,
    2001" and "The South Tower"
Hiram Poetry Review: "Notes from the Temple"
Hudson Review: "The Shadow Racers"
Italian Americana: "China in Italy"
Laurel Review: "The New Bed"
Limestone: "Horse Girl"
Literary Review (U.S.): "Shells"
Oracle: "In Vain: Chekhov Curses a Production of *Uncle Vanya*"
Permafrost: "Passovers"
Prairie Schooner: "Dorothy, Middle-Aged" and "Einstein's Bellhop"
Roanoke Review: "Object Lessons"
Snakebird: Thirty Years of Anhinga Poets: "An Atonement," "The Nest,"
    "St. Peter's on the Mountainside," and "Terra-Cotta"
Southern Poetry Review: "Hard Water"
Staple NEW Writing (U.K.): "Nocturne with Revolver"
Weber: The Contemporary West: "Gold Panning on the Arkansas River
    near Leadville, Colorado"
Yankee: "Harvest Home, Northamptonshire, 1644"

"Hard Water" was reprinted in *Don't Leave Hungry: Fifty Years of* South-
ern Poetry Review (Fayetteville: University of Arkansas Press, 2009). "A

Scholar's Suicide" appeared in my first book, *Conversing with the Light* (Tallahassee: Anhinga Press, 1988) in a much earlier version. I hope that I have got it right this time.

I wish to acknowledge the contributions of those who have made a difference.

I am grateful for the support provided to me by the Ohio Arts Council (via an Individual Artist's Creative Writing Fellowship); to the National Endowment for the Humanities for my inclusion in multiple Summer Seminars or Institutes, which inspired much of the work included in this collection, especially the 2006 NEH Summer Institute: Venice, The Jews, and Italian Culture; and to Mary de Rachewiltz for inviting my family to stay at her castle, Schloss Brunnenburg, in northern Italy during an earlier NEH Summer Seminar.

In grateful memory of those without whom I wouldn't have gotten to this point: Archie Ammons, Nan Arbuckle, William Matthews, my parents, and, yes, Hollis Summers, who, thirty years ago, sent me on a quest to rhyme "Tuesday" with "fishing."

In gratitude to those who continue to make a difference: David Baker, Shaul Bassi, Murray Baumgarten, Marilyn Carder, Dana Gioia, Kevin Hearle, Maria Ignatieva, Sean Lause, Robert Morgan, Robin Russin, Reg Saner, Sergei Task, Henry Taylor, Gavin Wells, Morgan Wells, Norm Williams, and most of all, my wife and best critic, Ronda Healy.

Many thanks go to Kala Maehlman for her assistance in the preparation of this manuscript.

Thanks to Thomas Lynch for seeing the merit in this collection and to David Sanders and the rest of the staff at Ohio University Press/Swallow Press for helping me hone the collection and present it to its best advantage.

"Non è mondan romore altro ch'un fiato
di vento, ch'or vien quinci e or vien quindi,
e muta nome perché muta lato."

*The world's clamor is no more than a breath
of wind, which, whether it goes here or there,
changes names because the place is changed.*

(Dante, *Purgatorio*, Canto 11, 100–102, author's translation)

Contents

II

I.

Ping-Pong with the Nazis

Bored couriers have kicked off boots and set
their pipes aside, a Dutch interior.
The slapped ball clacks over the table
like a telegraphic code, then trickles
like faint hope across the marble floor.
How quickly he bends to retrieve it
and puts it back in play, the Jewish boy
living with false papers in a villa
owned by his mother's Gentile friends, and now
commandeered by retreating Germans
as divisional headquarters. The young
blond soldiers, deferential to a social
better, muss his blond locks like the kid
brothers back in the fatherland, like big
brothers steeped in genial menace.
He begs another game, so they relent.
As the ball resumes its chatter across
the no-man's-land strung with a net,
he calculates the risk that each shot brings.
And so do they. He holds his pee and serves.

Hard Water

The pipes shudder and spew a tainted stream.
Hard water. My mother seems to keep
it like a sabbath: tub baths one inch deep,
rigid towels, and tea with flakes of scum.

On my infrequent visits, I submit
to her economies. Widowed ten years,
she's tightened habit down till few can bear
its torque, still unwilling to admit

age greases us to loosen and let go.
She repeats an elegy of bills, the costs
depleting her. But her scrapbook insists
on my success: clippings and class photos

pressed under plastic, for history is prone
to fray or crumble. Our conversation
is a dust disturbed, motes of words that turn
a moment in the light, here and then gone.

A radio preacher's voice drawls between us,
praising devotion as "a golden chain."
Ours is forged by dint of drips, the stain
under faucets spreading its gospel of rust.

Side by side, we stand at the kitchen sink.
She scours each piece of family silverware,
and I, in turn, dry with elaborate care,
at home in the exiles we cannot forsake.

Last Peaches, Chalfont St. Giles, 1665

Ask for this great Deliverer now, and find him
Eyeless in Gaza at the Mill with slaves,
Himself in bonds under Philistian yoke.

(John Milton, Samson Agonistes, 40–42)

How easily a knife can cleave their flesh,
which ripened, gaudy emblems of the sun,
each fevered summer day as plague raised
dark fruit under armpits and at the groin.
White grubs lie cradled by the peach stones,
bedded in soft sores of purpling mush.
So rudely bared, they ball themselves
against the sting of sunlight and fresh air.
I pare them from their paradise of glut
and cast them down, alms for hungry jackdaws.
John sits and broods, his blank gaze fixed
on Gaza. He mouths a kind of Hebrew,
harsh consonants and the sullen cud
of rhetoric, an old man's outrage.
With doubtful steps and wavering resolve,
I come to him, dreading his displeasure.
He should not dwell on pulling temples down.
September's gasping gadflies fur the air,
and things will topple of their own accord.
I stroke his lanks of hair and invite him
to share a sweetness plundered from the worm.

Horse Girl

The Appaloosa's mane is snarled with burrs
       and stems, a tapestry of straw,
       bachelor's button, and briar rose.
One waifish eye peeps out like an urchin.

My daughter, Morgan, who sports a horse's name
       and temperament, is gentled here
       by her own firm brushstrokes that tame
each tangled strand, toiling all afternoon.

When she smacks its burly neck, the head swings
       round, a moment sated lovers share
       when the laying on of hands brings
ease without desire. To curry favor

takes on meaning I never knew before.
       Her radio supplies a ballad
       as she leans into the shoulder
of this slow dance with something larger.

Terrace on the Val Venosta

For Alma, Al, and Vance

All up and down the deep-cut valley,
church bells mingle hours in the timeless air,
and the bantam rooster, cooped behind
the grocer's stall, perks up and answers back.
Altars commanding awe, the Alps close in
as heat haze obscures one peak at a time,
like Haydn's symphony where each musician,
subtracted from the melody, rises, bows,
and exits, till orchestra goes solo.
Under walls stenciled with saints, sun-gilded trout
stir up halos in the holding pond and glide
toward resurrection in garlic butter.
Next door at Villa Maria, the plastic Virgin
in a wall shrine crammed with votive candles
collects loose change and a garland of wildflowers.
Tsk, tsk, tsk; huge sprinklers cool the crops,
a soothing scolding, as plums deepen,
Merlot grapes grow musky, and summer's clock
runs down. The Suevi farmed these slopes
before the Romans, lungs so strong they learned
to yodel, a faith so ripe they worshipped
spirits moving through the wheat and in the stream.
In such a place, one god does not suffice.

The Persistence of Memory: Houston, 2001

Sounding its comforting call, bathwater
lulls each child in turn, till five are dipped
and laid on the bed like tomorrow's wardrobe.

The bodies must be patted dry and dressed
in pajamas with elephants or clowns.
Damp, crew-cut hair glistens in brushstroked

highlights. How easy to mistake it all
for a classic Norman Rockwell scene.
The mind resists when horror laps the cream

of domesticity. On this canvas
children are curved into melted clocks,
and time, for a moment, shudders and goes limp.

The furnace whirrs its song of self-content,
conditioning air, conditioning ease
like a mother humming in the kitchen.

1962

I. In Ohio

Nine years old, I am living on Elm Street,
a boulevard shaded by lofty trees
whose twisted roots support warring factions
of ants. The sidewalk is my Iron Curtain
where I stomp the red ones into debris.
Next year will bring Oswald and Dutch elm disease,
but not worse than this. Downstairs, my father
displaces despair with a bomb shelter.

Ambiguous chore for a doctor sure
two shelves of Campbell's Soup will not cure
radiation sickness. But we'll die together,
spooning cream of mushroom. His good soldier,
I carry cement blocks to help him
raise our shrine, our bunker, our mausoleum.

II. In Moscow

For hours, Irina labors on a table
under a clock, learning to measure time
in increments of pain. Though it must double
as air-raid shelter, the cavernous room
has small, high windows to a sky alive
with clouds. She swallows fermented berries
to feed her cramps, and as the clock nears five,
fruit and fate enact their conspiracies.

At last the urge to push, and the gush
of blood and amniotic fluid. Then the baby.
In Ohio, my face begins to flush.
Do I hear a siren song? Maybe
the only bombshell that Russia has prepared
is this pert child. And I will not be spared.

An Atonement

Above the table, to ward contagion off,
an onion dangled and balled a fist.
Like playground bullies, dangers clustered
round your house on Rhodes Avenue, where I
was condemned to dine with disaster.
Beets so purple they bruised the plate.
Bars of halvah like sweetened plaster.
Jarred gefilte fish bobbed in murky brine
like sheep brains in the biology lab.
Butter beans like bullets soaked in slime.
Thick as axle grease, your apple butter
made me wonder what darkness had festered
good apples into ghoulish gobs of goo.
Raised in a world of burgers and fries,
I gagged on every course, and palmed
what I could into my slacks.
                              Forgive me,
Grandma Emma, for all I pushed aside—
the banquet of exile you offered up,
the bloated sour cream floating on the soup.

The New Bed

At last, after ten years of marriage,
a new bed where we raft the calm passage
of an uncommitted Saturday when children
drowse past eight. Our daughter barges in,
not quite awake, dragging her pillow
like a rumpled shadow. Our son follows,
haggling till we squeeze him in beside her.
Here is the flesh of our best adventures
in the creaky hand-me-down we carted
to Goodwill last week: the mattress spotted,
the weathered side-rails starting to split.
Gavin roots under our quilt, a rabbit
in the warren of our legs, while Morgan
feeds the hungry duck I shape with my hand.
Cast out from our private garden of lust,
we are tamed into keepers of this
menagerie. Last night, once they were asleep,
you came out for me, your hair all done up.
This morning, our daughter sways before us
in pagan dance, chewing an old silk rose.

Spring Fever

In memoriam Carlo Levi

As he bends over patients, their eyes darken
like the cripples in Masaccio's fresco
of St. Peter's shadow curing the stricken.
Clasping hands, squeezing ankles, he passes down

the dialysis ward, a cook testing pastries.
His pinch imprints the swollen skin, bodies
awash in the shipwreck of their kidneys.
So blood endures its separate sorrows,

shoved through an array of tubes and filters
at their sides, while they recline in a row
of lounge chairs, dozing under newspapers.
Though starched sisters frown, he opens windows.

A Tuscan spring pulsates Vivaldi—
girls in black dresses hike up their hems
and weave motorbikes down thronging alleys.
And the sun builds glittering palazzi

from the common wares of each market stall:
melons so supple that the hand is called
to pat them; satins and silks that smooth all
sulks and send a current coursing in the veins.

With such a summons, who would not blend in
with the crowd, to select some chianti
and try on new shoes? Permissible sins
in a garden of second chances, however brief.

Dirty Laundry

Desire fine-tunes these lovers to a hum.
Veiled by false errands, they manage to meet
here, two towns from home, to launder sheets
and bath towels from their rented room.
Like honor guards, they fold each item
to an embrace we make sure to ignore.
Whiffs of warm cloth domesticate this chore
and they inhale its elusive perfume.

As washers mutter suds, soap operas
flicker in the window of each drier—
slippers and slacks, underwear and bras,
clinging, coupling, letting go—brief affairs
of promiscuous cloth caught mid-writhe,
falling head over heels, tumbling dry.

Along the Troubled Shore

Cell phones aroused, they pace opposite sides
of the street, concocting lies for spouses—
their invented meetings in other states
almost over. "Home soon. Love you too."
The phones snap shut like triggered traps.

A resort town after season, Grand Haven
is the fact of their fictions. One last night
in a bric-a-brac bed-and-breakfast
so homey that they've forgone condoms,
daring circumstance to solve for doubt.

September wind salts lips and eyes as they
stroll, arm in arm, married in the minds
of any strangers who bother to look.
Trawlers slosh and bob in moorings strained
by choppy water. The pier creaks like springs.

As they kiss, Lake Michigan churns a tall
breaker the gap-toothed seawall chews to froth.
Soaked back to infidelity, they shake
as gulls indict their names, and each smashed swell
crashes back, dank water beyond its element.

Object Lessons

I once took pride in simple moves, the ease
of packing two steamer trunks and leaving
torn posters with tape stains browning through,
shelves contrived from boards and cinder blocks,
the ghastly plaid sofa bought at Goodwill
that induced psychosis or headlong flight.

Latest in a dynasty of keepers,
I now take my turn hosting holiday feasts
surrounded by heirlooms and acquisitions
that seem double-bound in my life's DNA.
Above a Stickley desk of quartersawn oak,
an Impressionist oil of Italy

centers me here. In the hutch, china plates
are stacked like coins, and, passing, I count
upon their jangle. Each vase strikes a pose
supple as a lover's hip. The longing
in belongings lines up in rows of books,
a thousand titles of how owned I am.

Young Retrievers: Near Oxford, 1973

I believe in keeping quiet if possible when a dog is retrieving, as this teaches him to return on his own initiative. Remember, later in life you will often be hunting in cover conditions.

(Kenneth Roebuck, Gun-Dog Training Spaniels and Retrievers)

At Bourton, a hunter tossed a stuffed glove
into the Windrush to see his three retrievers
beat the river into froth, repeatedly
competing for a prize they could not keep,
content to grasp the moment in their teeth.

You were the game bird I scrambled after —
the slippery prize to hold in my arms.
Afternoons at Blackwell's, I knelt before
the poetry shelf, a novice laying claim
to vacant space my books would fill. And you

crouched there, slim Buddha in blue jeans
seeking the Zen of Social Psychology.
Jew and nonbeliever, we tracked down churches
where you took solace in your diary
and I communed with monuments and brasses,

the resonant debris of other ages,
cool Latin like satin sheets for the tongue.
We did not have a brother/sister look.
But the constable who found us camping
near the road was polite enough to ask.

We woke once in a field, hedged in by heads
of massive cows munching our sleeping bag.
As we gazed up, sunrise flamed on the clubs

of hooves. The whole herd bunched and bullied us
to the fence, like barkeeps rousing drunks.

Beside the Thames, you jabbed your legs
at brown trout drowsing in the mossy shoals—
provoking tics of shadowed zigs and zags—
while I taught stones to briefly skip their fate.
Silt and portents vexed the undertow.

A pair of lovers training for the meet
of separate lives, we passed our trials,
sang our duet. Like broken-voiced choristers
in back pews, we shape those lyrics on our lips.
The voice that doesn't sing perfects itself.

The life that isn't led invents itself,
pacing quadrangles with echoing steps.
On evenings when a boy and girl escape
the cloister for the linden grove, it whispers
from the Isis of was and cannot be.

The Traveler from Porlock Makes
a Journal Entry, July 1797

> *At this moment he was unfortunately called out by a person on*
> *business from Porlock, and detained by him above an hour, and*
> *on his return to his room, found, to his no small surprise and*
> *mortification that though he still retained some vague and dim*
> *recollection of the general purport of the vision, yet, with the*
> *exception of some eight or ten lines and images, all the rest had*
> *passed away like images on the surface of a stream into which a*
> *stone has been cast.*
>
> *(Samuel Taylor Coleridge's notes on "Kubla Khan")*

Mr. Coleridge seemed much distracted,
like one roused abruptly from a dream.
He signed the papers I had prepared for him,
though his pen hung like a frozen cataract
above each signature, shaken in his hand
as if drawn elsewhere like a water wand.

I tried to catch his interest by describing
the lightning strike on St. Dubricious spire
and the trout run under Porlock Weir.
But his eyes rolled as if he were imbibing
swigs of scrumpy at the market fair.
His busy fingers laced his rumpled hair.

I'll wager he had taken laudanum,
for he would mumble broken sentences
under his breath, describing caves of ice
and brightly clad throngs and cavalcades come

to honor Kubly Can, or some such like.
So I bundled his papers and resumed my trek.

A whiff of opium powder must have strayed
the air of his close, candle-sputtered room.
For, against my will, all the way home
my mind was plagued by images that played
out pagan pleasure domes and roaring streams
of flood. Please God they someday quit my dreams!

Visiting Grandma Emma

I. A Peasant in the A&P

She stubbed her thumb in every chicken,
her police blotter of suspects
for supper. Unabashed immigrant
in a red babushka and farmer boots,
she elbowed into lines and spooked
the checkout girls, denouncing the rise
of coffee prices and the fall of France.
Straying as far away as she'd allow,
I let my foot provoke the sliding door.

II. The Rest of the Cast

Fresh from her latest divorce, Aunt Lara
laid a minefield of spiteful notes concealed
under place mats or behind photographs.
Upstairs the invalids who boarded there
were spoon-fed helpings boiled until taste
was a memory of youth. Emma made sure
to garrote a tea bag for ten straight cups,
looping the string around, pulling it taut.
They rarely lingered beyond six months.

III. Bedtime Stories

I fidgeted at the end of her bed
as she brushed and braided her hair,

a red anaconda to strangle dreams.
As Akron's late-night sirens battered
the window, she told how her cousin
was shot against the garden wall
for rolling bad grapes under hobnail boots.
Once she tucked me in, I'd hear her
prowl the house, keeping out *les boches*.

IV. *Nights in Her Attic*

Up from under warping floorboards,
the world would snort and catch its breath
and hold that breath a bit too long,
a shuffling column of sound that would
detonate, and, after a pause, seize more breath
while my throat clutched mine like treasure.
Trunks with odd markings loomed round the cot
where I held fast and rode out the night.

Unsettled Accounts

. . . earth, no heavier
with me here, will be no
lighter when I'm gone: sum or
subtraction equals zero.

(A. R. Ammons, "The Account")

I dwell in country leveled by ages
of ice. Fields abhor contour, contrary
to the nature of Nature to rumple
the plain and jumble the ordinary

at regular intervals. Sifting through
stubble for thawing cobs, Canada geese
bark at my husky, who tilts back his head
and howls the Pleistocene behind my house.

Against this backdrop, Archie's death won't sum.
In Ithaca, his Cascadilla Falls
runs an adding machine whose roll never
needs to be changed, and never totals.

Here, sun reduces ice to puddles
on patio slate wiped clean as losses mount.
Departing geese form part of an equation
clearly greater than anyone can count.

Dance Lesson: Oakland Veterans' Memorial Hall

My feet are like a Picasso portrait
that gazes in too many directions.
The injured instructor kindly explains
that the two-step actually has three steps,
though I take four, none of them quite right.

Measured feet should be my second nature,
but I lift when I should slide and shift my
weight unevenly. My dance partner's eyes
run horror footage like when the creature
lurches from the swamp. Which way will I veer?

Will she spin out of control? Will my next
misstep drag her down, her body plundered
chicken coop to my voracious foxtrot?
As I switch partners, both of them sigh —
one in relief, one already perplexed.

My daughter brought us here from Berkeley
to her haven from stress, but ground zero
to mine. Her grace defies her parentage.
She took some pains to guide my fledgling steps
then turned me loose to whirling destiny.

Halfway round the dance circle, my spouse
has been swapped to the protective arms
of a stranger less likely to dislocate

her hip. In parody of my dating years,
I stumble through every embrace.

Just outside this gothic hall, Lake Merritt
glitters like a dance floor strewn with stars.
In thirty years or so, I will perfect
my tango there when East Bay breeze blows in,
lithe as my last breath, slinky as a ferret.

In Venice Ghetto, 2006

For Shaul Bassi

If Venice changes us, it's as a thirst
that can't be quenched, a thread that tangles
etymologies, where the sea insists
on the fundamental and the *sottoportego*
tunnels to new light. In one yellow campo
shaped like a badge, walling in and walling

out are balanced on wooden pilings
a thousand years old, allegedly
immune to decay. Green shutters are closed
to eyes and afternoon, and muffle praise
the cantor utters on the highest floor
where prayers rise like heat or are scrawled

and dropped, frail boats on the boundary canal.
Across the stone pavement, soccer balls spin
between boys careful to avoid the shrine
where Auschwitz is whispered
under a marble tally of deportees.
And still the hidden Jew defies all counts.

The rabbi burnt his list of congregants
and swallowed poison, allowing time
for most to escape to new identities.
Survivors in the Hebrew Care Home toss
and turn against Adriatic swelter
as the fan intones, "*Baruch, Baruch.*"

In this city that passes and passes,
Vivaldi's scruffy heirs ply their bows, cases
open to coffer coins bystanders toss.
From every third shop window, masks return
our stares, forged passports at a price.
And yet we cannot bring ourselves to leave.

Here, where languages blend into babble
and, for an instant, babble rings clear,
we find haven. Along a narrow chute
called Calle del Forno, our voices mingle
with the crowd, and *impade* cakes reward
a taste for exile, a hunger for home.

Lovebirds

We bought a pair for Morgan's Sweet Sixteen,
cheap sentiment wrapped in tropical squawks.
Morgan has turned, in the years that intervene,
to martial arts that can split concrete blocks
or crowd-surfing the mosh pit at raves.
Having murdered his mate, taking pains to strip
her skull, the tattoo-winged male survives,
a screeching green fist to pummel our sleep.

In his only escape, he blundered
our jungle of banisters and lamps. He lit
on the mantel and meekly surrendered
when we snagged him with a butterfly net.
He bangs his cage like any death-row thug.
And who can blame him? He was framed for love.

The Jewish Cemetery on the Lido

For Murray Baumgarten

At night, under wraps, often none too soon,
the Ghetto gave up what it must—bodies
rowed in silence across the long lagoon.
Bora winds scattered dust on canvas
shrouds intended to disguise Venetian
Jews as freighted cargos—to ward off spit
and stones. Dust and water, all the ablution
Venice would bestow, faceless behind
its marble masquerade, enforced oblivion.

On the Lido's sandy waste, they found
the graves which they were not allowed to own
in parcels of unconsecrated ground
sanctified by troubles they'd endured.
Monks collected rents from families bound
to pay until Eternity when, according
to the rants of blood-eyed friars, their kind
would swelter in fire to pay Hell's rent.
Till then, the slow assault of gale-blown sand.

Cautious carvers labored to invent
tombstones with Hebrew walled in by Baroque
and heraldries no noble would resent—
scorpions for Copio; roosters for Luzzato.
When Napoleon needed convenient
targets for his firing range, these stones sufficed.
Turned upside down, they doubled as pavement.
With his defeat, those duties were relieved
and families guessed at rearrangement.

Today in this tree-shuttered enclave,
we come to parse inscriptions, searching for
a past that punctuates our lives.
In Venice, *La Serenissima*, city
apart from everyday earth, these graves
define a separate district of apart.
Outside the obscure gate, sunbathers thrive.
From the busy street, no one spares a glance.
Hidden still, these dead have managed to survive.

The Nest

A bandaged mask woven by paper wasps
mutters treason from the garage gable's crest.
Unsteady
        on the stepladder's forbidden
top platform, I lift a broom to swat it
far enough to insure my safe retreat.
When my hard swing
            misses,
               gravity
grabs my shoulder,
            commanding allegiance.
Tumbling,
       I improvise
          a triple twist
and tuck
       onto the driveway
           which applauds
my skull.
       Tottering on one leg,
            the ladder
rocks back with amplified force,
           and topples
onto me.
       From a befuddled jumble
of scrapes and sprains,
         I gaze up,
           unmoving.
Hairy with angels, the sun hums to itself.

Stung

In the seizure of summer running out,
a hornet stung her lip and shattered
their picnic by the lake. Then the welt of doubt—
her husband home with a life that still mattered.
And him, toasting fifteen anniversaries
in Stratford, laughing with a loving wife
at Falstaff's botched adulteries.
A sudden inflammation in his left eye,

blood backwashed in the cornea like a tear
too big to cry, too burning to ignore.
Thus pain revoked their holiday from care,
and let them taste, like Lancelot and Guinevere,
how the tongue thickens with each deception,
honey and venom compounded into one.

Padova Pilgrimage

Tony, Tony, turn around.
What is lost shall soon be found.

(Childhood rhyme invoking St. Anthony of Padua)

An elementary school classmate assured me
the rhyme would work, if only I'd believe,
and I'd avoid spanking for another lost glove.
Instead I fumed and took my punishment.

I'm still an angry Jew, partly appeased
by Giotto and gelato, Italy
at its best, blending fervor and flavor.
And there, eloquent in its reliquary,

St. Anthony's mummified tongue and tonsils
said to attest his sweet voice and sermons
that compelled the fishes dancing from
the stream and magnetized all that was lost.

If I believed, my God would be Old Testament
but ironic, petrifying the source
of Anthony's tirades against the Jews.
I insert my coin and light the bastard up.

Arbeit Macht Frei

With daily weeding, Emma imposed race codes
on crabgrass, from knees that knew no begging.
As if the blades of her front lawn had cheeks,
she pulled and pinched till they were plush
and edged like a regiment at drill.
If only they hadn't wished to kill her, she would
have done the Germans proud with work that made
her free like the motto her relatives passed
under, one way, at Auschwitz-Birkenau.

An immigrant, she had found refuge in
America, but something less than freedom.
Ignoring screams in languages they could
and couldn't understand, Akron nurses took
her firstborn, Elsvetta, to be sterilized
for Down syndrome. When her young husband died,
in-laws came from states away, while she was
sewing in a sweatshop, to inspect her
daughters and abduct her sons. She got them back,
but honed her faith in imminent disaster.

She took revenge on dust and backyard chickens,
which she beheaded with a gusto
that prompted Mom to dub her Robespierre.
Fluent in French, German, and Yiddish,
she battled English, unable to distinguish
between *holocaust* and *roller-coaster*.
So she did her best to shield grandchildren

from amusement parks with their well-guarded
entrance gates and promised horror chambers.

After Elsvetta died, aged fifty-four,
at the Apple Creek Asylum near Wooster,
a gestapo of guilt kicked in the door
of Emma's heart. Now her old neighborhood
quarters a new kind of ghetto. Yellow
crime tape marks where crystal meth and shattered
panes inflict a belated *Kristallnacht*
on the home she kept painted and polished
to postpone the knock she always knew would come.

Last Judgment in Ferrara

Angels prod seven naked sinners chained
together by their crimes. Pigeons mock them
with excrement and the flapping of wings
while God broods, impassive on his throne.
From the marble portico, all gape down
as demons stir a vat of the damned
and season it with another soul, there
on the cathedral's storybook façade.

From a café below, I return their stare,
sipping tortellini broth and Emilia wine
to mute the restless canticle of flies
like rumors of misdeeds I am sure
to pay for—betrayals and jealousies;
a passion for the palace of horrors
known as history. A shudder born
of humid air animates carved figures
with all the choices I ought to regret.

Across the street, Savonarola stretches
bronze arms wide, conjuring a bonfire.
Over his shoulder, the fortress towers
where Browning's last duchess died for a smile
and partisans and Jews were displayed
after interrogation. Yet when Blackshirts
torched Ferrara's synagogue, a German
officer dodged past the mob to rescue
ritual scrolls that he smuggled home

and spent a lifetime mending. Scholar
of second chances, he labored unaware
a damaged Torah must be burned.

The synagogue survived, still Orthodox,
so women must squint like God's auditors
through the high gallery's ornate shutters,
lest they be unclean or spark temptation.
I would have joined them, had it been allowed,
to study scorch marks on the blackened beams—
the only Hebrew that I can decipher.

Instead, a minyan of one, I loiter
in silent congregation with the damned
and saved; the saviors and tormentors;
and their stone-certainty. I raise my glass
to celebrate all unsettled accounts.

II.

The Shadow Racers

Two girls, one boy, and the August doldrums.
All too soon, they'll follow in the turning
wake of combines long past sunset, inured
to grit and grain till the harvest is in.

Their Kansas farm too far from playmates
and oceans, they improvise a tag with light
and shadow—long afternoons when fleets
of clouds are driven over summer skies.

Sliding from the fence once the sun is blocked,
they drop onto the pasture's yielding grass
and race the surge of sunlight, a breathless
all-out sprint to safe haven on the porch.

The light will swamp them if they're caught
in between. Then they must float face down,
teased by weeds that any gust can coax
to swells unless new shadows break the spell.

From the white porch deck, the rail fence rises,
a shoreline beckoning castaways.
Eager to embark, they lean from the steps,
freighting dark cargo they cannot declare.

St. Peter's on the Mountainside

A temple
          stood here
                    before the Romans,
its changing
          gods crushed
                    and reborn as grapes
in arbors
          on the terraced slopes
                    below.
Though dry rot
          pocks and scabs
                    the frescoed saints,
one glance restores
          their gaunt,
                    ferocious grace.
Difficult to budge,
          the oak door
                    tugs open
to reveal
          St. Peter,
                    who fingers a key
and stares back
          with unflinching
                    eyes of soot.
St. Margaret's cross
          has swelled
                    to skewer

the sheepish dragon
                    lolling
                              at her feet.
Crowned
          with a wheat sheaf,
                              and wounded
with carnations,
                    Christ endures
                              the cudgel.
Suffering defies
                    abstraction,
                              where lambs
are hung
          and gutted
                    in the shed outside.

Camping with Jarrell

And after he has taken off the thoughts
It has taken him his life to learn,
He takes off, last of all, the world."

(Randall Jarrell, "Field And Forest")

Randall went with me down Bright Angel Trail,
backpacked in with tent and cooking tins—
utensil for the mind, his volume thick
enough for a headrest, a raft for dreams
wedged under my bedroll that night.
By morning, damp had bled his later
poems into a gibberish of ink blots,
free associations that cost three ninety-five.

Eroding iron streaked cliff walls red,
a crime scene eons old. Armadas
of schist and sandstone sheared through waves of time
as the swollen Colorado swayed
its boa against earth flesh, white water
churning into froth, the elemental
striptease. I opened the pages that were not
stuck together, to read and reread them

like river on bedrock. But when my raft
flipped on a boulder, his book bobbed out
of my keeping, dodging a traffic of rocks.
Perhaps a hawk swooped, reflected,
and veered away. Perhaps some poems snagged
on the crowbar of sunshine that pried
the canyon further open, diverting
a darker channel, never finding bottom.

Gold Panning on the Arkansas River
near Leadville, Colorado

For Ronda

Just downstream from the ranger tower,
sculpted bedrock curves to a sheltered cove,
scooped out by floods, overhung with sage.
There, where turbulence loses its load, we delve.

In this gulch edged by cliffs, the eddy is
unruffled though the stream goes frothing by.
Old rhythms, new to us, grow familiar
in rich desolation under mountain sky.

I shovel from long-settled deposition,
not boulders, ordered with compulsive care,
not stones in matched, diminishing pairs,
but gravel, sand, and silt closer to shore.

Your pan rocks like a cradle, inviting
current on one side, sloshing it out the other.
You thumb out the dross, umpire of what is
worth saving from each trial by water.

In the bottom of your pan, liquidity—
bits of pyrite, gold, and mica compete
brightly for the sun's (and our) attention,
our challenge, simply to discriminate.

Greed, not for wealth, but for the task itself
compels us here from jobs done to the clock.
Dubbed by sunlight, you kneel to a motion
beyond our own, a past we've taken back.

China in Italy

Rock scorpions curl into ideograms
along the Via Ezra Pound. Chickens roosted
in a battered sedan are scratching out
Confucian odes in the road's summer dust,
that temple scroll eternally revised
by what passes, including me with my copy
of *Cathay*. Any river merchant's wife
could stand and muse by these unpainted gates.
An imperial barge of sun shimmer glides
down the Adige toward Verona.
Halfway up the steep slopes, a shawl of mist.
Graziella, barefoot in the morning,
slips to the pond with a bucket of bread,
singing to herself. Noisy ducks converge
to parse the grammar of crumbs on water.
A few sure strokes on a rice paper screen
sets this scene five hundred years ago.
Marco Polo traveled east in error.
China was always much closer to home.

A Scholar's Suicide

In memoriam John A. Jones

On your last trip to Cambridge, you fled
the station platform in sudden dread,
desperate to light one final candle
under the arches of King's College Chapel.
Already at loss for your life, you ran,
your heart's fugue confirming no return.
To see for myself, I have come.
Carved marble hovers like sheltering palms
over that cool and radiant harbor of hymn
where Tudor lyric rides on boys' unbroken
voices. It's your inflections I imagine.
Your seminar was a salon
with Dryden, Pope, and Dr. Johnson,
as I plied Boswell's trade, each couplet
sipped and savored like a good claret.

An eighteenth-century scarifier
was that well crafted, but scarier.
A subtle spring would trip the hidden blade
and open up a vein, like wit displayed,
the tooled leather case still faintly pink
with hasty blood. And so I think
of you, of healed scars that keep
the body's journal, of Johnson's quip
that he was too large of girth
to make a single course for death.
His bleedings were a style of dying,
a swan song frequently reprised.

The gun to the temple was a resolve
more awful than Sam Johnson's. I grieve
less for the family you didn't introduce
than for the books which lost a voice
that still could chant their delicate,
demanding songs. For Swift's quick wit
and Pope's relentless pulse, I have brought
your news to Cambridge, a carried tune.
With my candle, I sing it to the stones.

Einstein's Bellhop

I. Energy

Trying to manhandle his own scuffed cases,
he seemed, at first, an immigrant peddler
misdirected to our marble reception.
But his frizzed hair, that brain power perm,
gave him away, and I answered the bell.
"Welcome to the Windy City, Mr. Einstein.
Let me handle those." They were heavy, full
of old wool, old world. "Got your formulas
all packed?" He just stared like a simp
at the parallel universe of his shoes.

II. Equals

Do geniuses tip? He turned the key;
I followed him in, put down the bags, tuned
the radio. Stood there. Started to go.
"A moment, wait." With a grimace, he
switched off Les Brown and his Band of Renown,
fingered the stand for excess atoms,
tested both faucets, and flushed the toilet
twice, gazing down the spiral galaxy
of water big banged to Lake Michigan.
"Is good." He handed me a crinkled one.

III. Mass

In just eighteen months, he was nothing
that mattered, a convention of molecules
checking out—leaving keys on the bed stand,
sheets to be changed, no forwarding address.
Two weeks later, my father, a boiler man,
pulled out his hankie, swiped at a sweat
that wouldn't go away, and keeled right over.
Gone just like that, massive in his absence.
Like a trolley engulfed in fog. Only the flash
and sputter of sparks to tell of its passing.

IV. Times

pass. Les Brown, Dad, the real Mayor Daley.
Trolleys, cage elevators, radios with tubes.
Starched white shirts, bow ties without a clip.
Once upon a time, it seemed appropriate
for old men to die, making room for me.
I'd roll the top down and ride my roadster,
destiny, untouchable as Al Capone.
Now when the desk clerk shakes his head and sneers,
I know the score on relativity.
Live long enough—your life's an elegy.

V. The Speed of Light

He said that time and space are twins.
And both can be outrun. My legs ballooned,

I sprawl in the lobby, inert all afternoon.
Water stains island the ceiling's map.
A mushroom cloud suspended, the chandelier
takes aim. Our plumbing wheezes its burden,
part concertina, part soul in torment.
As my space closes in and my time runs out,
the twin I never had smirks to himself,
traveling nowhere at the speed of light.

VI. *Squared*

At the speed of light, time loses track of itself
and stops its mutter of eternal now.
It rides the express of already over/
hasn't yet begun, enfolded in space,
consumed, assumed, like the pickled herring
that swam downstream on Einstein's breath.
I tell you, I was his bellhop, and that counts
for something. I open my right hand
to was, is, will be, and wait to see
if the final tip will scald my palm.

The Lion at the Fountain

For Mary de Rachewiltz

The lion abides at the fountain,
features blurred by centuries of wear.
A tower cocking a fist, Castle Fontana,
Schloss Brunnenburg. In a canvas chair, a man
grizzled, word worn, sighing for *Tchi*
under the dolomite shadow of Tschigat.
" . . . would prefer a small mountain temple."
Snails tack their sails, straight up the wall.
Fish drowse and dart in the fountain pool.
Let them be koi. Let this be China.
It ought to be China. Wind batters the glass.
West wind and oblivion's dust. Goats graze
terraced slopes. Ought to be China. Surely
the lion was a palace dog, carved jade
before this alabaster Romanesque.
Archangel Michael raises scales and judgment sword.
Broken into beauty, when the lion roars,
its voice will be Kung. And the fountain goes on. . . .

Passovers

Larimer Street supported five and dimes
and tailor shops with rolls of gabardine.
Mr. Stone, the balding Jew who rented rooms,
cautioned all visitors to leave a bribe
for the dybbuks, soul-snatchers who accept
socks or a pocket comb, little ransoms
to buy safe passage to an intact home.

He'd left such tokens at Bergen-Belsen.
Assigned to the camp commissary,
he diverted moldy bread and barley soup
from the slated-to-die to those with some
chance of survival. For each lined name,
he yanked one hair, his pride and special
vanity, to keep his own uncrossed.

Later, refugee in a cowboy town,
he dropped that name, Stern, which replayed
a numbered past best concealed by long sleeves,
for one more enduring and apt to blend in.
A fossil collector, he turned himself
into Stone, amazed that time could jewel
death into quartzite instead of soap.

His Seder was frugal: borscht, gefilte fish
and matzoh-ball soup, served up with wine,
one glass for him, and one for me, and one
for the Prophet Elijah, which he stashed

outside the door, bloody handprint to ward
off slaughter. Once I moved on to marry,
he sent a card for each anniversary
with the phrase *Much luck* scrawled in red.

They say his body went unclaimed for weeks
and was consigned to a potter's field
bounded by a refinery complex
that belches smoke like a crematorium.
And so, tonight, I choose to think it's him,
not wind, ruffling the surface of the glass
outside my door, his eyes a mist of gas
swirling among nameless, numbered stones.

Feuds

In the faded parlors of Tirolo's two best houses,
the widows still duel at their pianos.
Something like Schubert turns the swallows
into notation, circling unresolved.
Slugs tryst listlessly to the answering
strains of Chopin, waltzing at dirge tempo.
High on an outcrop, a *castello* shakes
its crenelated fist at the tower one ridge over.
Stinging nettles defend the granite walls.
At each arrow loop, the quick salamander
or the scorpion with barbed tail flexed,
a *Gabbiano* warrior in chain mail.
Under them, the Adige runs to meet its lover,
Isarco, and on to Verona where lovers die.

"Crazy-bucks"

In memoriam Emma Selzer

Ages seven to nine, when chance and size
aligned, my cousins and I stuffed one
of us into the laundry chute that slanted
from the hall of Grandma Selzer's second floor.

Lightning bolts provoking the thunder
a body makes careening in sheet metal,
we explored a space beyond the bounds,
like NASA astronauts, and tumbled

from its maw onto piles of stiff clothing
arranged to cushion our hard landing.
Shaking off the daze, we stumbled to hide,
though we'd be found and made to pay the price.

The cellar bin, its oozing rubble walls
painted cyanide blue, would be our cell
when Emma thumped downstairs to round us up
at broom-point. Her cousins had been gassed

and stuffed in ovens by a rocket-building
master race. She shook her head, "Crazy-bucks,
Meshuganah," and latched the door against
flesh of her flesh so tempted by its fate.

Terra-Cotta

Five hundred years in the making, this
ramshackle Tuscan farmhouse continues
to accrue levels, with sheds and goat pens
mortared into rooms. Its kitchen flagstones
readily compose baroque variations
on footsteps long gone. Burnished flowerpots
attest the subtle chemistry of sun
and time — as art relaxes and wears down
to a more enduring, elemental form.
Once moss and lichens are factored out
and two thousand years of rain factored in,
a Roman legion wends its way across
the crackled contours of a marble chunk
haphazardly patching the garden wall.
My finger follows them to victory
and sentry duty above tomato poles.
Each fruit hails Caesar with its ripe palm.

Live Fire

He towed me, quivering, across the pool
as my fingers gouged deeper in his leg.
I clung like an aquatic koala
determined not to sink or swim.

Still he labored extra laps, resigned to
prepare me for Naval Basic Training's pool
of fire, its surface coated with burning
kerosene while bursts of bullets wrinkled

the air above. He knew safety depends
on swimming under flame. At seven,
I knew it depended on resistance.
When he kicked to dislodge me, I drew blood.

He'd swum once from a sinking ship
and expected mine would come. In the locker
room, old soldiers sloshed over to display
thick, zigzag scars for his approval.

I dropped my gaze from them and from his
scratches, not cowardice exactly.
In our hall closet, I ignored warnings
to stand inside the braided dress white jacket

that hung there under cellophane, its chest
of ribbons a semaphore proclaiming

how he'd borne a scalpel into battle
to undo the damage war had done.

But in the deep end of nightmares, old wounds
reopened to suck me in. Awake, I
cringed beneath the fire of expectations—
unfit to swim or bear the sight of blood.

In Vain: Chekhov Curses a Production of Uncle Vanya

"Thus, knowing nothing, uncultured, very clever, and unusually
important, consumed by envy, with an enlarged liver, yellow,
gray, bald, I prowl from house to house, give the tone to life, and
everywhere bring something yellow, gray, bald. . . .

"'Ah, what boredom!' I say in a despairing voice. 'What oppressive
boredom!'"

(Anton Chekhov, "In Moscow," trans. Louis S. Friedland)

What oppressive boredom! I'm sick to death
of this whining. Vain, in vain, Vanya—
how sorrow conjugates itself in endless
repetitions. Wouldn't a waltz and the swish
of petticoats make better entertainment?
Instead these creeping yellow vapors haze
every corner of the house, and linger
like a burned supper to haunt the cook.
This stench of sweet decay consumes my lungs
quicker than tuberculosis, and more galling.

I recall one production of *The Sea Gull*
where, as Sorin prattled on about Moscow,
the ash on his cigar grew impossibly long.
The actor, who attended him, hesitated,
waiting for its fall. It grew longer.
And right on cue, as he lifted Sorin,
the glowing ash fell, branding his forearm.
A method actor, he barely winced. Ha,
the night's best drama artfully concealed.

Can this equal that? These actors act
like they haven't read their parts. Here's Vanya's pistol.

Live ammunition would play a fine prank.
Or else rehearse them in a solitary cell
and starve them till they're willing to trade
Stanislavski for a slab of old meat.
Or spit gobs of blood, anything to break
the spell of life in Russia's provinces,
parched for the *petits jeux* that sparkle
in each glass, even when the wine is flat.

Catching Lizards near Vicenza

For Robin Russin

The path skirts a stone wall embroidered
with ivy and mottled lizards that stitch
the crevices in afternoon heat. The first
few escape, ruffling dry leaves into taunt.
Then Robin removes his Panama hat,
allowing sun to burnish his bald spot.
A Botticelli page with masses of hair, Ben
drives them to the slapped hat. Robin runs
a hand beneath and brandishes each catch.
Sarah, wife and mother, shakes her head, more
baffled than upset by her husband,
the tenured scholar, gone sudden thirteen
with the heat haze and cricket concerto
halfway up the hill to La Rotunda.

Notes from the Temple

I.

The flooding Arno managed to dissolve
Cimabue's crucifixion scene waist high.
So the scholar knelt in muck to retrieve

paint flecks, and thus restored Christ's simple needs—
new legs already nailed, no half reprieve
from pain. Lumbago and sore purple knees

rewarded those labors after a life
of monographs, meetings, and faculty teas.
His tweed demeanor disdained the gaffe

of girls who scroll-worked nearby balconies
with bras and pastel underwear as if
to disconcert the *quattrocento* frieze.

II.

Returned to Ithaca, where students sprawled
inert in rows, he claimed that statues
by Praxiteles could roll down College Hill

unharmed, "a column concealed in each pose."
Carole quipped, "Then he should take a tumble."
Slide after slide detailed cracked Apollos

while my tanned hand crept up her supple
and consenting thigh, a survey of arts
more to our liking, there, in the Temple

of Zeus, cramped among Gods plaster cast.
More eternal than marble, we were tempted
to hack them to pieces. Who needed the past?

III.

Decades later, I browse among antiques,
attentive to style, patina, and glaze —
caressing each find to feel what it speaks.

There is much body in a thing well made,
a charming damage betraying its age,
since edges will tatter and surfaces fade.

Boccaccio lists the treatments for plague —
powdered emeralds in wine or gold dust pastes,
treasures traded to placate fever's rage.

An icon with dry rot is shedding flakes
of gilding. I dab one against my tongue —
the tang of centuries, an acquired taste.

Nocturne with Revolver, Moscow, 1930

See how still the world has grown.
Night has laid the sky under a tribute of stars.
In such an hour as this, one may rise and address
the ages, history, the universe.

(Mayakovsky, "Unfinished Poem #IV," trans. Daniel Weissbort)

The lamp spurns its shadow and he stirs tea.
Grief and stale fish soup unsettle his gut.
He lifts a revolver to his lips and plays it
like a flute, his part in the symphony
of pill bottles, razor blades, and dangling ropes.
Drunks at dockside watch old freighters sway.
Husbands and wives, in pairs, are lying in state.
Still, and double still, the night has grown.
Roosters and hens are mating in their coops.
They'll be plucked in market stalls at dawn.
At this hour, the dead congregate, and the living
grow uneasy. Crimes fester and come knocking
while hopes diminish to a muffled note
and dreamers writhe on the flypaper of dreams.

Duet

For R.L.S.

In the Pyrenees that June, summer opened
like a book of hours. Basque reapers askew
beside gilded haystacks, raising wineskins.
The woodcutter's laden cart paused below—
the donkey grazing, the driver blowing rings,
his smoke borne into haze that slowly blued

the valley. Beneath the ridge, we found
a ruined chapel, properly medieval,
whose tracery windows were glazed with nothing
but sky. A battered stool and bits of wool
betrayed its latest flock, so lately sheared
and sent to market. Inside was cool.

Our boots on flagstones summoned buried notes.
Unpacking your harmonica, you gnawed
the hardtack of ballads: "Shenandoah,"
"The Way We Were," and "Yesterday," each flawed
rendition suffusing a sorrow sure
as Roland's, and as ours that followed.

But the horn of separation was still
unsounded, the blows of battle not yet struck.
With my tin whistle, I retorted with jigs
for you, for us, and for the wind which took
both burdens, in counterpoint, toward France,
scrolling the margins of our temporary luck.

Past Midnight, I Soak My Feet, Ravenna, 1317

> "You shall leave behind every delight
> which you hold most dear; this is the bolt
> that the bow of your exile first gives flight.
>
> "You shall learn how like the taste of salt
> is the bread of others, how like a hard street
> to tread the stairways of a stranger's court."
>
> (Dante, Paradiso, Canto 17, 55–60, author's trans.)

Damn this place! The bakers salt the bottom
of the loaves, raising a thirst that wakes me
in the small hours, parched as any glutton
who sucks an empty cup in endless gloom.

I spare myself two swigs of tepid water
from my jug and douse the rest upon my feet.
The aftertaste of sulphur makes me shudder—
Devil's piss filtered through Ravenna's wells.

Bruises on my soles record the sorry tale,
a heraldry of calluses, badges of my travels
up and down the Apennines, from exile
to exile, a *purgatorio* of plods.

Treading the smooth stairs of a stranger's court
makes arches ache worse than the round basalt
that paves old Roman roads. They still run straight,
a taunt to those who follow crooked ways.

I watched one afternoon as men tore down
a granary from Cacciaguida's day. Rats seethed

from its foundations till the street, which ran
its narrow course between the rat man

and his bony bitch, was cobbled with motion.
They swarmed to his swung spade, fearing metal
less than fang and growl. Their dying squeal
denounced the fate that harried them from home.

Baser than those rats, Florentine factions
scurry to the flags of silken fellows
adept in dishonor and deceit: Guelfs
and Ghibellines who would shame a gallows.

Yet, at sunset, the towers and chimneys
of Firenze were sainted by a glow.
The muddy Arno would ripen to a field
of light that visions fluttered through.

These days, I feed the fleas where it pleases
my patron to send me on errands, places
where any glimpse of paradise grows dim.
Like an old gelding, I nod in my traces.

I must pinch the candle and go back to bed;
the mattress, bunched and hard, is molded
to another's shape—someone who had
his uses and came at the Duke's command.

In the vastness of sleep, my toughened soul
retraces stony paths, each one forsaken.
I cannot seem to rub it soft again
between my palms. Perhaps God can.

Harvest Home, Northamptonshire, 1644

A distant column of smoke staggers up
a bruised sky, troopers burning the ricks.
Yet her son, pressing cider, martyrs only
windfalls. Her daughters teach the cream
to clot so it can crown her shortcakes.
For the gleaners, she has made provisions:
one dull knife, a joint of sauced mutton,
gravy for sops, and ale by the gallon.
She'll send them home sated so none begrudges
the eight dozen apples under her bed,
the cheeses her husband suspends from each beam.
The bread ark holds a testament of loaves.
Scrolls in a tabernacle, a day's baking
spreads the gospel of plenty with every whiff.
The bulk of the harvest is hidden or sold
with famine and battle a full county off.
Aglow with such luck, she lays the table,
turning its smooth boards upside down.

From Jerusalem Hill

"For certain it is a promised land. I want it."

(Sir Walter Raleigh, after falling from his horse at first glimpse of Sherborne)

Spotlit against encroaching dark, Sherborne
Castle glows like a tended hearth, its gates
stark firedogs. I trespass on this hill
whose view commands the valley, and the will
of passing travelers to trade a place
at court for its repose. From slopes below,
moos and shuffling hooves challenge my presence
crunching through brambles or scaling a fence.
Carved on market hall and almshouse row,
the Digby motto, "In God, Not Fortune" —

the latest tenant's boast and cattle brand.
September storms have felled another cedar,
leaving, of the grove that Walter Raleigh planted
from Virginia seeds, four to be supplanted.
Despite chainsaw and headsman's axe, Sir Walter
flaunts these proud heads at a buried king.
And sap still rises to the stump, the tap root,
snarled in stubborn marl, sending up a shoot.
The hourly London train goes clattering
its workaday refrain, yet here I stand

where Raleigh tumbled onto Dorset loam.
He scrambled up, bespattered and bemused
by the fortunes he would need to spend
to mend his garments and somehow befriend

the Bishop of Salisbury, who, he supposed,
would, for the right bribe, relinquish the field.
Home is a heraldry that wish invents
from soil it promises itself, monuments
it chooses to erect. As headlights gild
its pockmarked walls, his house calls travelers home.

Indigo

In memoriam Lina Brock

A shade to memorize, not quite purple,
the enigmatic I in ROY G BIV.
Then, one evening in Santa Cruz, you
led me to a bin of Moroccan cloth
and traced my fingers over dust devils
of dye until they were smudged with musk,
an aromatic print of North Africa.
Wedded to desert sweat, indigo rules
the pores in ways no French soap can subdue—
a nomad's irreducible essence.
Tuareg, as you chant its poems, crackles
like insect husks sucked for moisture
when sand is anvil to the sun, its word
for summer a barely stifled yell.
You fold a mottled scarf in your handbag
like a map or tent, what you can carry
of years in the Sahara, a nosegay
of caravans and Berber market stalls
where you sniff the color of wandering.

Dorothy, Middle-Aged

Grape-colored clouds on the skyline
decant their storm. Soon it'll pour.
And I will, too—Jack Daniels black,
enough to float three cubes and make
them clink, like Auntie Em's false teeth
plopped safely in a bedside mug
as she snored up my worst night sweats.
I plink my nails against my glass,
an echo and an exorcism
of ruby slippers when Kansas
was a wish.
                      Now the storm veers south,
its wrath of wind resolved, or else
reserved for someone else. I spent
my luck in bringing home a man
who had no heart, no brain, no bravery
worth rousing, and didn't mind the lack.
Yet some huddled hack in the wings
of me pulled every lever
on the grand contraption of love.
I slosh another liquid dose
and try to sing the Munchkin song.
My voice, like a stuck phonograph,
falters over a single line,
"Because, because, because, because . . ."

The Final Toast

"I am dying. I haven't drunk champagne for a long time."

(Anton Chekhov's last words)

The doctor who cannot cure himself stares
as his failing breath shivers the surface
of a dram of champagne, and gulps it down,
wine transforming to fatal hemorrhage.

As his actress wife changes into mourning,
the cork in the unfinished bottle
thumps out—a cue she interprets as "tomb."
A black moth batters at the window pane.

Since death unsettles flighty clientele,
the manager of Badenweiler Spa
has the corpse stowed in a hamper
for discreet carting to the railway depot.

The baggage clerk checks his inventory,
the only coffin in stock, a child's.
So limbs are broken and contorted to fit,
one passenger who won't complain! There's space

in a refrigerated car marked OYSTERS
which is greeted in Moscow by honor guard
and military band dispatched to the wrong
platform to mark a field marshal's return.

Bedraggled seagulls forage between rails.
The playwright scripting this denouement

irons out the death of an ironist
with brass fanfares and undiscovered pearls. . . .

A dark blur flutters over spilled champagne.
When a maid opens the window to air
the room, something barely brushes her wrist,
more a yearning than a kiss, then rushes east.

Heaven and Hell in the Arena Chapel

For Michael Thaler

The sanctuary's barrel-vaulted sky
bends toward blue eternity, though rows
of frescoes run the length of both walls—
market stalls that broker good and evil.
Mike identifies icons and credits
early reading lessons from a worn *Lives*
of the Saints owned by the Polish couple
who risked their lives to shelter him
while his parents hid from Nazis
in the forest, a Biblical story
which Giotto would have painted well.

For Giotto understood the mysteries
of transformation. A lamb contemplates
the leap to Paradise. An angel peeks
from behind a tree. Satan gnaws sinners
as a line awaits the justice of his jaws.
Once we exit, we scavenge the gift shop
for cards to carry home an aftertaste
of his ravenous Hell. Only Heaven
is on sale. The cashier's sneer betrays
assumptions. Nonbelievers challenge her
convictions. Others have mistaken us
for father and son, somehow united
by the holy ghost of being Jewish.
In Akron, where I'm from, I hid
behind my Gentile father and surname,
blending in so well that open hatred

takes me by surprise. Like Joachim's backward
glance at the temple door barred against him.

Giotto also stood apart. A Tuscan
shepherd boy till Cimabue found him
scrawling on a stone, he lacked for social
graces, but not for patrons willing to pay
the canny bumpkin with the steady eye
and a hand sheep-dipped in something
like miracle. The sky that spans
his Chapel is the one he measured
from the fold. His Hell-scape unsettles
anyone who has bedded down wary
of predators or the whims of pestilence.
As we leave, sunlight daubs a fleeting fresco
through shrubbery while buses lumber past.
Scents of cedar and diesel fumes contrive
the mixed message that we all must parse.

Hearing the Beat

Before it meant sunrise, dawn was the note
of hooves on Rhodes Avenue brick. The dray horse
that pulled the milk wagon clopped out a code
of content, its route a known universe.
Those moments, weightless between the poles of dark
and day, I felt a vast, incessant hum
till trolley wheels lathed up whorls of spark,
that gnashing engine on its leash of time.

Half a life later, the Big Bang echoes
on radio telescopes, the original splat
blurting its energy across the cosmos.
Somewhere in Akron's spreading slums, I plot
its center among catalpa and wild rose —
a boarded-up dairy where bees drive dynamos.

The South Tower

In memoriam Richard Beech

For an instant, those floors took the shape
of the second airliner, like a belly
when a fetus turns. One who would escape
looked on as flaming bodies fell,
a live performance of *Paradise Lost,*
their impacts like bursting bags of plaster.
He stood, dumbstruck, till commodities of dust
charged the streets, a bull market of disaster.

He rose, with other victims, a ghost
of old Pompeii, wrenched from daily business
to watch the world end, and calculate its cost.
As he surveyed that sudden abyss,
a sheet of paper fluttered down, a note
of termination, unsigned and rendered moot.

Shells

In memoriam Cora Mayhew Wells

Those evenings of my grandmother's cancer
meant playing alone in the hospital lobby
as my parents read and prayed for her
and she muttered back her delirium.
I deployed toy soldiers on linoleum,
ready to do battle. An old farmer
shuffled over one night to inspect them.
From his bib overall pocket, he extracted
my reward, a handful of .22 shells,
tiny brass casings to shoot like marbles.
So I sent them pinging off chairs and walls
in wars truer by their burnt powder smell.

Twice a week, the doctors would alternate
drafts of chemistry and radiation,
a regimen of poison to placate
the ravenous cells that fed on her.
Dad led me upstairs to say good-bye.
A wraith on morphine, she kept calling
for her husband, a gassed grenadier
dead for decades. She gripped my hand,
repeating, "It hurts me, Will." Confused,
renamed, I gave the only pill I had.
She puckered her gray lips and drew
a sweet lost love from a lozenge of brass.

Putting It Together

For Ohio winters, I paved the floor
with that jigsaw puzzle—a cobbled street
winding past whitewashed houses with flowerpots
and tile roofs to an alcazar, my childhood
cipher of Europe, no location named.
Once it was assembled, I'd whirl barefoot
on a thousand bright pebbles of elsewhere
till I'd fall, drunk with almost being there.

Thirty years flit by like seagulls in sun,
shearing the dazzle. On a travelogue,
ladies in mantillas climb that cobbled lane
in Portugal. And I am back upon
cold linoleum with cramping legs,
turning the final piece as if it can
unlock the blocked trapdoor through time and space
and guide me home to every foreign place.

Notes

Ping-Pong with the Nazis

I am indebted to Leo Jesorum, a holocaust survivor, who shared this story with me in 2006.

Last Peaches, Chalfont St. Giles, 1665

In addition to the epigraph, this poem appropriates and adapts one line from John Milton's *Samson Agonistes*, which was composed in Chalfont St. Giles while Milton and his new wife took refuge from the outbreak of the plague in London. This poem's speaker, Milton's third wife, Elizabeth, was twenty-six years old in 1665; John was fifty-seven and blind. The Puritan elders had selected Elizabeth to be John's "helpmate" because of her sweet disposition and extraordinary good looks.

The Traveler from Porlock Makes a Journal Entry, July 1797

Divining rods are known as "water wands" in England's West Country. St. Dubricious is the parish church of Porlock, noted for its tall spire. "Scrumpy" is hard cider produced in western Somerset near Nether Stowey.

In Venice Ghetto, 2006

My favorite entrance to the Venice Ghetto is via the *sottoportego*, a combination tunnel and bridge, which allows the visitor to climb from darkness into the bright light of the Ghetto's central campo (that is, piazza). The story of the chief rabbi's suicide is true. *Impade* cakes are specialty pastries unique to the Venice Ghetto.

The Jewish Cemetery on the Lido

Venetian Jews were forbidden burial on San Michele, Venice's cemetery island. Instead they were forced to use a more distant sand spit, the Lido, now developed into Venice's beach resort. Although Napoleon liberated the Venice Ghetto and bestowed citizen status on Venetian Jews after 300 years, he also looted their cemetery.

Padova Pilgrimage

Giotto's masterpiece is his Arena Chapel (a.k.a. the Scrovegni Chapel), Padua's greatest artistic highlight. Padua's artistic lowlight may be the chapel in the Basilica of Saint Anthony, where it costs one euro to view St. Anthony's mummified tongue and tonsils. And, yes, in spite of his sainthood, Anthony's writings reveal a fierce anti-Semite.

Last Judgment in Ferrara

Savonarola was born and educated in Ferrara. A statue across from the cathedral depicts him in the midst of his harangue on "The Bonfire of the Vanities." Ferrara's dominating castle was home to the d'Este family of Robert Browning's "My Last Duchess" and served as a gestapo headquarters and prison during World War II. On the other side of judgment, a young German officer risked his life to rescue the Torahs from Ferrara's burning synagogue.

Einstein's Bellhop

For what little I know about the Big Bang theory, thanks to Kim Malville at the University of Colorado and Carl Sagan at Cornell University. I also thank fellow scholars Tim Redman (University of Texas, Dallas) and David Heaton (Ohio University) for stories about their chance encounters with Albert Einstein, and fellow poet Roald Hoffmann (Cornell University) for the story about his hotel stay before receiving the Nobel Prize in Chemistry. All blame for this poem is mine alone.

The Lion at the Fountain

I am deeply indebted to Mary de Rachewiltz, poet in her own right and translator of her father's *Cantos* into Italian, for her hospitality in allowing my family to stay at her castle, Schloss Brunnenburg, in northern Italy and for permitting my access to her father's private library and her private clippings file. Tschigat is one of the Dolomite peaks that overlooks the castle. Tchi is one of Kung's companions in "Canto XIII" and speaks the line quoted in the poem.

Notes from the Temple

Former students of Archie Ammons will recognize some details of the Temple of Zeus in Cornell University's Goldwin-Smith Hall and be baffled by other details. Former art history students at the University of Colorado (CU-Boulder) will recognize some details of the Flatirons Theater and be baffled by other details. Both universities stand atop a steep College Hill. The poem conflates details from both locales to create a fictive third locale, though surely someplace lovingly known as CU. Fortunately neither university owns an original Praxitiles, or I might have subjected it to Dr. Alden Campbell's proposed test.

Nocturne with Revolver, Moscow, 1930

Rumors persist that Mayakovsky did not commit suicide, but, instead, may have been "assisted" by the KGB.

Past Midnight, I Soak My Feet, Ravenna, 1317

Ravenna was Dante's final place of exile. Cacciaguida is Dante's grandfather, who serves along with Beatrice as Dante's guide to Paradise.

From Jerusalem Hill

Jerusalem Hill in Dorset overlooks Sherborne New Castle, the home that Sir Walter Raleigh built during one of his exiles from Elizabeth's court. Upon Raleigh's execution, the home was purchased by the Digby family, who are still in residence.

Indigo

This poem was inspired by the late Lina Brock, anthropologist and translator of Berber poetry, a fellow scholar at the 1988 NEH Translation Institute at the University of California, Santa Cruz. The Tuareg word for summer is pronounced "Yell." That knowledge completes my Tuareg lexicon.

Heaven and Hell in the Arena Chapel

A series of frescoes chronicle the life of Joachim after his expulsion from the Temple, whereupon he took up the life of a simple shepherd, essentially a life in reverse of Giotto's.